Read About Birds

ONE

What is a Bird?
Beaks and Feet
Nests and Eggs

O. B. GREGORY

Illustrated by Elsie Wrigley

 WHEATON A member of the Pergamon Group

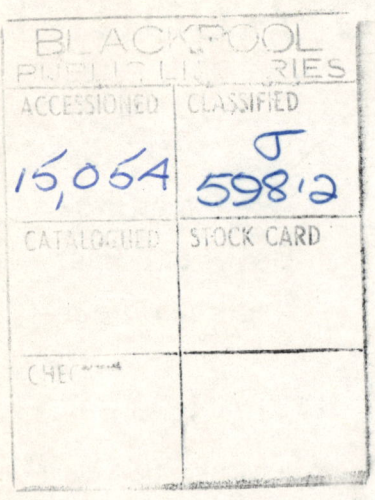
© O. B. Gregory, 1973

This edition first published 1973
Printed and bound in Great Britain
by A. Wheaton & Co., Exeter

ISBN 0 08 017679 8

CONTENTS

WHAT IS A BIRD?

What is a bird?

A bird is an animal with feathers.

Most birds can fly,
    but so can bats and insects.

Birds lay eggs,
    but so do many reptiles.

But the only animals with feathers
    are birds.

Feathers are useful to a bird.

They help to keep it warm.

They save its skin from getting wet.

They help the bird to fly.

Sometimes the colours of the feathers
help to hide the bird.

Sometimes a bird uses its feathers
to line its nest.

Birds spend a lot of time
looking after their feathers.

The picture shows a jay preening itself.

Some birds are quite naked
when they hatch from the eggs.

The feathers grow later.

Other birds are covered with down
which is soft and fluffy.

The picture shows a young bird
that has just hatched out.

Its feathers will grow later.

A small bird such as a wren
has about two thousand feathers.

A big bird such as a swan
has about twenty-five thousand.

All birds have two legs
and two wings.

But not all birds can fly.

The penguin and the ostrich
cannot fly.

The penguin uses its wings
as flippers or paddles.

They help it to swim.

The ostrich can flap its wings
but they are too small
to lift it off the ground.

Most birds build nests.

Some birds go to a lot of trouble
to make a nest.

Others do not make much of a nest.

They use a hollow in the ground
or a ledge on a cliff.

The cuckoo does not build
a nest at all.

It lays its eggs
in another bird's nest.

The picture shows a blackbird's nest.

All birds lay eggs
and all birds hatch from eggs.

Some birds lay only one egg.

Some lay up to twenty eggs.

Most of our common garden birds
lay about five or six eggs.

They hatch in about
two or three weeks.

Some chicks can run about,
but other young birds
are quite helpless.

This is the most dangerous time
for the young birds.

Thrush

Mallard chick

Birds are warm blooded.

This means that their body temperature
is always the same.

Their usual body temperature
is higher than ours.

They are very busy creatures,
flying, hopping, running or swimming

They use up a lot of energy.

This means that they must
eat a lot to keep going.

All birds do not have
the same shape of beak.

This is because they do not all eat
the same kind of food.

They do not have teeth
to help them break up their food.

Kestrel

Chiffchaff

Seagull

Robin

Chaffinch

Moorhen

Mallard

All birds have a backbone
and a skeleton.

The bones are small and thin,
but they are very strong.

The long bones are hollow
which keeps the bird light.

Birds have strong muscles.

More than a third of a bird's weight
is muscle.

Birds need strong muscles
to beat their wings.

Most birds have very good eyesight.

Birds of prey, such as eagles and hawks, have the best eyesight.

Owls' eyes are different
because they both look in front.

Birds have ears, but the opening
is usually covered by feathers.

As well as allowing a bird to hear,
ears help it to keep its balance
when it is flying.

Birds can taste what they eat
but they do not usually have
a good sense of smell.

Tawny owl

Birds living in the wild
do not live very long.

Most small birds live for
between two and six years.

Birds that live in captivity
live longer than those in the wild.

Canaries kept as pets may live for
twelve or thirteen years.

Parrots and ravens have been kept
for more than sixty years.

Budgerigars

BEAKS AND FEET

Different birds have different shapes
    of beaks and feet.

We can tell quite a lot
    from their beaks and feet.

We can tell something about
    what they eat.

We can tell something about
    how they move.

The front limbs of a bird
are its wings.

They are used for flying.

So its beak must sometimes
do the work of hands or paws.

A bird uses its beak
to find and pick up food.

It uses its beak to feed its young.

It uses it for preening feathers
and for making nests.

A bird may also use its beak
to defend itself.

The hawfinch has a short, thick beak.

The hawfinch eats seeds.

Its beak is useful
    for breaking open the seed cases.

The pied wagtail eats insects.

Like most insect eaters
    it has a thin, pointed beak.

The eagle eats small animals
    and birds.

Its strong, curved beak
    is good for tearing flesh.

Hawfinch

Pied wagtail

Eagle

The crossbill has an unusual beak.

The upper and lower parts of it
are crossed over.

The crossbill eats the seeds
of pine cones.

Its beak is useful
for getting the seeds out.

The woodpecker's beak is strong,
sharp and pointed.

The woodpecker eats insects
that bore into tree trunks.

So it needs a strong, sharp beak
to peck the bark and wood
to get the insects out.

Crossbill

Woodpecker

The curlew has a long, curved beak.

The curlew spends a lot of time
    on the sea shore.

There it pushes its long beak
    into the mud and sand
    looking for food.

It eats shellfish, sandworms
    and other small sea animals.

The shoveler is a kind of duck.

Its beak is wide near the tip.

Inside the shoveler's beak
    there is something like a comb.

This is used to sift water and mud
    for insects and worms.

The heron eats a lot of fish.

It wades into the water,
    keeping its neck curved.

When the heron sees a fish
    it shoots its neck forward
    and catches the fish in its beak.

The goosander also eats fish.

Inside the goosander's beak
    there is a row of little lumps
    like the teeth of a saw.

These "teeth" point backward
    so that a fish will go in
    but not slip out.

Heron

Goosander

The picture shows three birds
that have unusual beaks.

The puffin's beak
is red, yellow and blue.

Some of the colours disappear
in winter.

The puffin uses its strong beak
for catching fish.

The spoonbill pushes its beak
into soft mud and water.

It feeds on water plants, fish,
water animals and insects.

The razorbill has a white line
across its beak.

Puffin

Spoonbill

Razorbill

The legs of different birds
are well suited
to the way they live.

Most birds have three toes in front
and one behind.

The woodpecker climbs trees.

So it has two toes in front
and two behind.

They give the bird a good grip.

The robin is a perching bird.

It has three toes in front
and one behind.

Most water birds have webbed feet.

But all their feet are not webbed
in the same way.

The picture shows four different kinds
of webbed feet.

They belong to these birds:
great-crested grebe
coot
mallard
gannet.

Eagles have very sharp claws.

The claws are used to pick up
small animals that eagles eat.

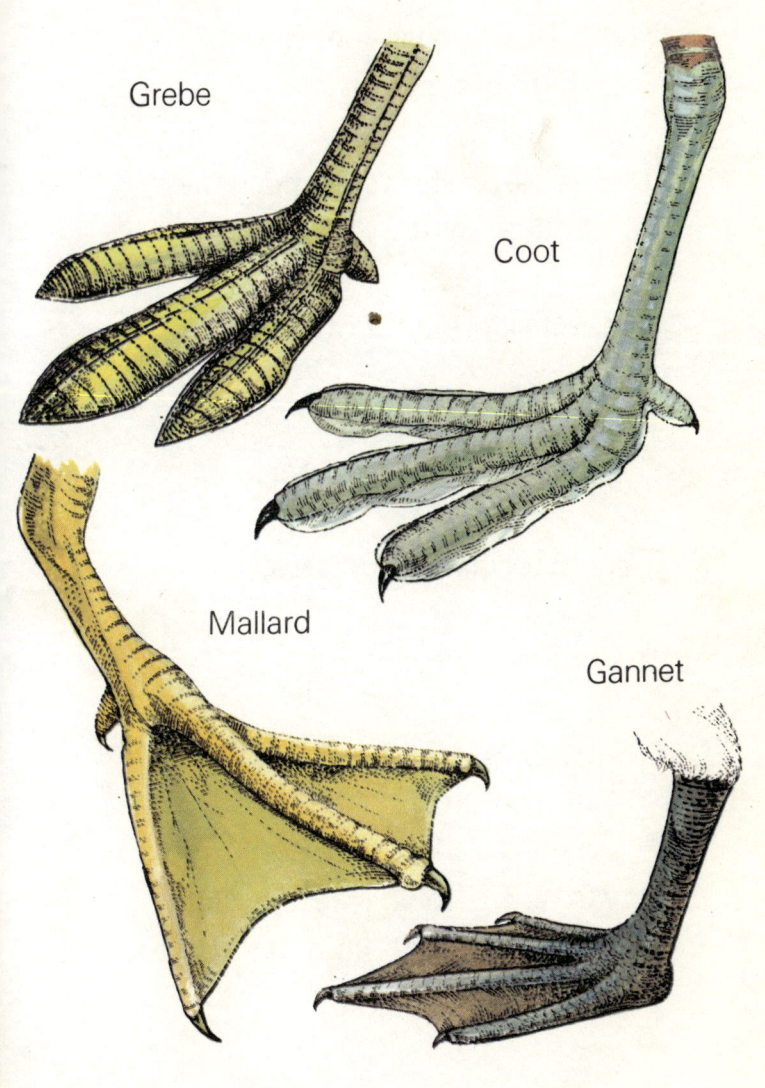

Grebe

Coot

Mallard

Gannet

Some birds have longer legs
than others.

The picture shows a redshank
and a swift.

The redshank is a wader.

It needs long legs
for wading in water.

The swift has short legs.

It does not need long legs.

It spends most of its time
in the air.

It can cling to a tree or wall
but does not land on the ground
very often.

NESTS AND EGGS

Most birds make nests.

They make nests to lay eggs in
   and to hatch out the eggs.

The nest is often used
   as a home for the young birds
   until they can fly.

A nest is not usually a home
   for all the family.

It is not big enough.

Most nests are made of dry grasses,
leaves, moss, hair and wool.

But some birds use other things
as well.

The kingfisher uses dry fishbones.

The song thrush lines its nest
with mud.

The house martin uses mud
and not much else.

Rooks and crows use mostly twigs.

Ducks and geese line their nests
with down.

The down is used to cover the eggs
when the birds are away.

Kingfisher

Song thrush

House martin

Some birds nest in colonies.

A colony is a lot of nests
close together.

Puffins nest in colonies.

They find some soft grass
on an island or cliff.

The bird makes a tunnel
and its one egg is laid there.

Gannets nest in colonies.

The colonies are usually
on a rocky coast or island.

Gannet colonies are noisy.

Sometimes the birds fight.

Sometimes they take each other's eggs.

Some birds make wonderful nests.

The reed warbler builds its nest
among reeds growing in the water.

The nest is shaped like a deep cup.

It is made of grass, moss and wool
and is built round the stems
of two, three or four reeds.

The long-tailed tit
makes a domed nest
in a bush or hedge.

The birds go in and out
through a hole in the side.

Some birds do not make
  much of a nest.

The guillemot lays its egg
  on a rocky ledge.

The egg is pear shaped.

If it is touched
  it will turn round
  but not fall off.

The nightjar does not make a nest.

It lays its eggs on the ground.

They are marked with brown and grey
  and are not easily seen.

Birds that nest on the ground
often try to hide their nests.

The skylark always lands
a little way
from its nest.

Then it runs through the grass
to the nest.

The colour of a bird
often helps to hide it.

The male pheasant has bright colours
but the hen is brown.

When she is on the nest
she is not easily seen.

Every bird knows how to make
its own kind of nest.

The parents do not teach them.

No one teaches them.

They know by instinct where to build
and what to use.

Some birds come back year after year
to the same nesting place.

Eagles and swallows do this.

Swallows often mend the old nest
by adding fresh mud.

Not all birds' eggs are the same size.

The mute swan's egg is about
　　four and a half inches (115 mm) long

The goldcrest's egg is just over
　　half an inch (15 mm) long.

A cuckoo is bigger than a blackbird
　　but its egg is smaller.

A blackbird's egg weighs about
　　a quarter of an ounce (7 grammes).

A cuckoo's egg weighs about
　　half as much.

The cuckoo lays its eggs
　　in the nests of smaller birds.

It lays a small egg to match theirs.

Mute swan

Goldcrest

All birds do not lay
the same number of eggs.

Guillemots, razorbills, puffins
and gannets lay one egg.

Nightjars, doves and pigeons lay two.

The herring gull lays three.

Some birds do not always lay
the same number of eggs.

Starlings lay from four to seven eggs.

Pheasants and partridges may lay
as many as twenty eggs.

Razorbill

Partridge

All birds do not lay
eggs of the same colour.

Eggs laid on the ground
are often marked with spots.

The spots help to hide them.

Woodpeckers nest in holes in trees.

Their eggs are white.

The dipper makes a domed nest.

Its eggs are white.

The cuckoo's eggs vary in colour.

They are laid in other birds' nests.

They are laid one at a time,
each in a different nest.

READ ABOUT BIRDS

If you have enjoyed this book you will want to read other books
in this series:

1. WHAT IS A BIRD?
   BEAKS AND FEET
   NESTS AND EGGS

2. HOW BIRDS FLY
   MIGRATION
   GARDEN BIRDS

3. WOODLAND BIRDS
   BIRDS OF PREY
   SEA BIRDS

4. BIRDS OF COAST AND SHORE
   BIRDS OF LAKES AND RIVERS
   DUCKS, GEESE AND SWANS

Ask to see our Read About Nature series